STAN LEE'S LOVE STORY

...AS TOLD BY HIS
ONE AND ONLY DAUGHTER, JC LEE

STAN LEE'S LOVE STORY

...AS TOLD BY HIS
ONE AND ONLY DAUGHTER, JC LEE

FORWARD BY
STAN LEE

Stan Lee's Love Story: It's All About Love

Published by Fatsalagata

ISBN: 978-0-9961418-2-6

Printed in the United States of America

Author and Designer JC Lee

First Edition 2016
Second Edition 2023

Production by Klein Graphics, Concord CA

I ALWAYS FELT LIKE I CAME OUT OF
A BOTTLE OF COLOR FROM A COLORIST AT
TIMELY COMICS. THAT WAS THE NAME OF
MARVEL BEFORE DAD CHANGED IT. I REMEMBER
ONE CARTOON, POPO THE CLOWN, WHO CAME
OUT OF AN INK WELL. I REALLY HATED THE
CHARACTERS WHO EACH WEEK TRIED TO TRIP
POPO UP BECAUSE HE WAS THE STAR. I LOVED
THE COMIC BUSINESS AND ALL ITS COLOR.
THE ARTISTS HAD TONS OF BOTTLES OF INK
IN EVERY SHADE YOU CAN IMAGINE. BACK
IN THE DAYS WHEN I WORKED AT MARVEL I
WAS THERE AS OFTEN AS I COULD BE. I WAS
EXCITED BY ALL THE ENERGY AND CREATIVITY.

NOW I CHUCKLE AT PEOPLE WHO SAY
THEY CREATED A CARTOON OR CHARACTER OR
ANYTHING WITH MY FATHER. MY FATHER HAS
ALWAYS BEEN METICULOUS AND WOULD NEVER
LET ANYTHING PASS HIS DESK WITHOUT HIS
FINAL APPROVAL. HE ALWAYS KNEW THERE WAS
AN AUDIENCE, AND HE SO LOVES HIS FANS.

WHEN I SAW STAN WITH A GREAT
ARTIST (LIKE JOHN ROMITA), HE WAS ALWAYS
THERE STANDING ABOVE HIM WITH PENCIL IN
HAND POINTING TO SOMETHING HE WANTED
CHANGED. HIS GIRLS HAD TO BE DRAWN LIKE
MOM, SEXY, BUSTY, BEAUTIFUL AND BRITISH
WITH A TURNED UP NOSE. MY FATHER LOVES
BEAUTY AND THAT'S WHAT HE SAW IN MY

MOTHER. HE SAYS, WHEN HE DRAWS WOMEN, SHE IS THE ONE HE ALWAYS DRAWS.

WHEN HE HAD THE TIME, DAD WOULD PERSONALLY WRITE TO HIS FANS. HE USED TO WISH HE COULD DELIVER HIS RESPONSES TO THEIR DOOR HIMSELF TO MAKE SURE THEY RECEIVED THEM.

WHEN I WAS AT THE SCHOOL OF VISUAL ARTS, MAGAZINE MANAGEMENT (WHO OWNED MARVEL) PUBLISHED A MAGAZINE CALLED, "CELEBRITY". THIS WAS BEFORE "PEOPLE MAGAZINE" WAS EVEN A THING. I WAS GOING TO FILM SCHOOL, STUDYING THEATER AND TAKING PICTURES AT NIGHT FOR "CELEBRITY" AND WHOMEVER ELSE WOULD PAY. WASN'T I AMBITIOUS? FAMED PHOTOGRAPHER BERT STERN GAVE ME A NIKON CAMERA THAT HE STOLE BACK YEARS LATER. REST HIS SOUL, BUT HE MADE ME QUITE THE "IT" GIRL IN SCHOOL.

I WORKED IN LONDON ON THE FILM "JABBERWALKY" - FOR NO PAY MIND YOU. ERIC CLAPTON WAS THERE, AND I PHOTOGRAPHED HIM. HE SAID TO ME, "JOAN C LEE? WHAT ARE YOU A TAX ACCOUNTANT? WHY DON'T YOU USE JC?" SO WHEN I GOT MY SCREEN ACTORS GUILD CARD, I THOUGHT WHY NOT? JC IT IS! I HAVE BEEN USING JC EVER SINCE. BUT UNFORTUNATELY NOT THE S.A.G. CARD -

AT LEAST NOT YET. HOLLYWOOD IS WAITING
TO CAST ME AS A GREAT-GRANDMOTHER.

BACK IN NEW YORK, I WENT TO WORK
WITH MY FAMILY. IT FELT LIKE A SOAP OPERA
WITH A CAST OF CIRCUS FOLK.

ONE FOR ALL, ALL FOR ONE!

IT WAS A CIRCUS RUN BY STAN. AS I
GREW UP, I DID JOBS AROUND THE OFFICE.
MARVEL WAS A SMALL COMPANY WITH FEW
PEOPLE - A FEW VERY TALENTED PEOPLE.

IN THE XEROX ROOM WAS MY FRIEND
STU WHOM I WAS ALWAYS CHATTING
WITH. I LOVED EVERYONE THERE. THAT'S
WHY IT REMINDED ME OF A CIRCUS: TRUE
ENTERTAINMENT AND PASSION FOR ART.
EVERYONE LOVED WHAT HE OR SHE DID AND
LOVED DOING IT. DAD WAS THE RINGMASTER,
THE TRUE MASTER OF CEREMONIES.

WHEN MY UNCLE MARTIN SOLD THE
COMPANY, IT REALLY TOOK OFF. MARVEL
WAS MARVELOUS. MY FATHER WAS IN HIS
ELEMENT AND WORE HIS MANY HATS WITH
PANACHE - THAT'S STAN. A FORCE TO BE
RECKONED WITH.

MOM WAS THE STAR AND THE TRUE
TALENT. SHE WAS "MRS. STAN LEE" WITH HER
GRACE, BEAUTY, CHARM AND CLASS. MY DAD
NEVER STOPPED CREATING. I TAKE SPECIAL
PRIDE, HONOR AND DELIGHT KNOWING THOSE

ARE MY FOLKS. JUST KNOWING THEM IS A
PRIVILEGE.

WHEN I RETURNED TO HOLLYWOOD,
MOM AND DAD WERE ALWAYS THERE FOR ME,
STANDING BY ME. MY PAST AS AN "IT" GIRL
WAS LEFT BEHIND, BUT I COULDN'T CARE LESS,
BECAUSE GOD HAS BEEN SO GOOD. I HAVE
MY FOLKS STILL WITH ME IN THEIR 90S,
STILL ROOTING FOR ME AND EVEN ADMIRING
ME - THEY STILL SUPPORT MY MUSIC, ART
AND JEWELRY MORE THAN I CAN SAY. I AM
FOREVER GRATEFUL.

LOVE,
JC

FOR MY PARENTS, WHO LET ME ENJOY
LIFE'S GLORIOUS DANCE SO FULLY
AND WITH SUCH ENORMOUS GENEROSITY
IN GRANDIOSE STYLE.
I DEEPLY THANK YOU BOTH FOR YOUR
OVER-THE-TOP LOYALTY AND FOR
STANDING BEHIND MY OUTRAGEOUS ART
AND (SOMETIMES OUTRAGEOUS) LIFE
WITH UNWAVERING SUPPORT.
I LOVE YOU ALWAYS.

FOREWORD...

NOT ONLY IS MY LOVELY DAUGHTER A FINE ARTIST BUT, WITH THE CREATION OF THIS BOOK, I NOW REALIZE SHE'S ALSO A GIFTED WRITER AND EDITOR - BESIDES HAVING THE SUPERHUMAN AMOUNT OF PERSEVERANCE AND ENERGY TO SIFT THROUGH LITERALLY HUNDREDS AND HUNDREDS OF PHOTOS, MANY DATING BACK MORE THAN HALF A CENTURY, TO FIND THE RIGHT IMAGES FOR YOU, THE EVER-DISCERNING READER - BECAUSE YOU DESERVE IT.

IN FACT, IF ONE PICTURE IS WORTH A HUNDRED WORDS, THEN THIS BOOK IS AN ENTIRE UNABRIDGED DICTIONARY OF AFFECTION AND GOOD CHEER.

Y'KNOW, BEING LUCKY ENOUGH TO HAVE A WONDERFUL WIFE LIKE JOAN AND A BEAUTIFUL DAUGHTER LIKE JC, I'VE ALWAYS TAKEN A HAPPY MARRIAGE FOR GRANTED. NO MATTER HOW MANY DISAPPOINTMENTS OR FRUSTRATIONS THE OUTSIDE WORLD MAY HURL AT US - AND, LIKE EVERYONE ELSE, WE'VE CERTAINLY HAD OUR SHARE - NOTHING CAN OVERCOME THE SUPPORT OF A LOVING FAMILY. AND IF YOU HAVE ANY DOUBTS, *WE'VE GOT THE PHOTOS TO PROVE IT!*

FINALLY, AS I THUMB THROUGH THE PAGES OF THIS ADMITTEDLY PERSONAL BOOK, I CAN'T HELP BUT REALIZE THAT, *DESPITE ALL THE SUPERHERO STORIES I'VE WRITTEN, PERHAPS THE GREATEST SUPER POWER OF ALL IS - LOVE!*

EXCELSIOR!
STAN LEE

THIS IS THE STORY OF MY MOTHER AND
FATHER. IT'S A LOVE STORY ABOUT TWO
PEOPLE WITH AN UNQUENCHABLE LOVE FOR
EACH OTHER AND FOR LIFE.

THE SECRET TO MY PARENTS' SUCCESS
IS THAT THEY FOUND EACH OTHER. THE
BEAUTIFUL BLONDE JOAN BOOCOCK, MY
MOTHER, KNEW EXACTLY WHAT SHE WAS DOING
WHEN SHE CHOSE THIS MAN.

THOUGH MY DAD HAS GARNERED NUMEROUS
ACCOLADES, MARRYING JOAN, MY MOM, IS
STILL HIS GREATEST ACHIEVEMENT. FOR 67
YEARS, SHE HAS REMAINED AT MY FATHER'S
SIDE OFFERING INSIGHT AND SUPPORT.

MAY YOU ENJOY THIS BOOK AND HAVE IT
GIVE YOU A GLIMPSE INTO US LEES. MR. AND
MRS. STAN LEE ARE TRULY A REMARKABLE,
POWERFUL DUO. GOD BLESS THEM.

LOVE,
JC LEE

MY DAD...

STAN LEE WAS BORN DECEMBER 18TH, 1922,
IN NEW YORK CITY. HIS PARENTS CELIA AND
JACK WERE IMMIGRANTS FROM ROMANIA...

STAN LEE

STAN (LEFT) FILLED HIS BOYHOOD DAYS WITH ODD JOBS SUCH AS USHERING AND WRITING PRESS RELEASES AND OBITUARIES UNTIL 1939, WHEN HE BECAME A GOPHER FOR TIMELY COMICS, ALL THE WHILE SPENDING HOURS ON HIS SIGNATURE KNOWING ONE DAY EVERYONE WOULD RECOGNIZE IT.

AN AVID READER, STAN ALWAYS HAD A PASSION FOR STORIES WITH HEROIC LEADS AND ROLE MODELS.

EVEN AS A LITTLE GUY...ADORABLE.

LITTLE DID HE KNOW WHAT HE'D ACCOMPLISH...BUT ONCE I WAS BORN, I KNEW.

1940 - NEW YORK

JOAN CLAYTON BOOCOCK

BRITISH ACTRESS AND MODEL BORN TO HANNAH CLAYTON AND NORMAN DUNTON BOOCOCK IN ENGLAND.

GROWING UP, JOAN WAS SURROUNDED BY HER FAMILY'S LOVE AND HER TWO SISTERS, AND BEING BRITISH, SHE LOVED HER DOGS. WHEN JOAN DISCOVERED HER TALENT AS A MODEL AND ACTRESS, SHE RECEIVED A SCHOLARSHIP TO THE ROYAL ACADEMY OF ARTS.

ENGLAND WAS TOO SMALL FOR HER. SHE NEEDED TO MOVE TO AMERICA TO PURSUE HER DREAM. THIS WAS BEFORE HER DREAM WAS STAN.

TO THIS DAY, SHE CAN STILL MIMIC ANY ACCENT. SHE COULD READ THE PHONE BOOK AND YOU'D BE ON THE EDGE OF YOUR SEAT.

JUMP AHEAD TO THE PRESENT - SHE'S ABOUT TO DO HER FIRST WEBISODE VOICEOVER AT 93!

IN 1939, STAN'S UNCLE MARTIN HIRED HIM TO SWEEP FLOORS AT TIMELY PUBLICATIONS, THEN LOCATED AT THE MCGRAW-HILL BUILDING ON 42ND STREET IN NEW YORK, NEW YORK. IN 1941, "PUBLICATIONS" WOULD BECOME "COMICS", AND IN 1942, TIMELY WOULD MOVE INTO THE EMPIRE STATE BUILDING.

IN 1941, AT AGE 19, THE YOUNGEST EDITOR AND MOST ELIGIBLE BACHELOR IN NEW YORK CITY. HE WAS A LADY'S MAN WITH A BIG PEN AND BIG CONVERTIBLE, BUT HE HADN'T MET HIS BIG BEAUTIFUL JOAN BOOCOCK YET.

STAN ONLY HAD A YEAR TO ENJOY THE RESPONSIBILITY OF HIS NEW POSITION, WHICH WOULD BE IN THE BUILDING THAT BROUGHT DOWN KING KONG. WHAT WOULD IT DO TO SPIDER-MAN?

EDITOR-IN-CHIEF AT TIMELY COMICS.

IN 1942, HE LEFT FOR THE UNITED STATES ARMY...

STAN SERVED IN THE MILITARY FROM 1942 TO 1945 - AS A WRITER, OF COURSE.

HE WROTE MANUALS, SCRIPTED TRAINING FILMS, DEVELOPED SLOGANS AND EVEN DID SOME CARTOONING. HE WAS GIVEN THE OFFICIAL MILITARY TITLE OF *"PLAYWRIGHT."*

WHEN HE CAME BACK FROM DUTY, STAN SETTLED BACK INTO MANHATTAN AND HIS JOB AS EDITOR IN CHIEF AT TIMELY COMICS. HE ENJOYED A GREAT LIFE AS A BACHELOR AND A SUCCESS.

THE OFFICE WAS CONSIDERED MAGAZINE MANAGEMENT. TIMELY WAS OWNED BY A MAGAZINE COMPANY THAT OWNED MANY OTHER PUBLICATIONS - CARTOON, SEXY, SPORTS AND MOTORCYCLE MAGAZINES TO NAME JUST A FEW.

ONE DAY, MY DAD HAD A BLIND DATE AT LEIGHTON HATS ON 4TH STREET AND 5TH AVENUE IN NYC... MY MOM WAS NOT HIS DATE!

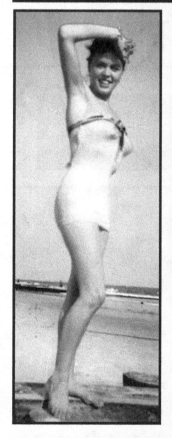

...AS LIFE WOULD HAVE IT, IT WAS MY MOTHER WHO OPENED THE DOOR...

ALL IT TOOK WAS ONE "HELLO" IN HER DEEP BEAUTIFUL BRITISH ACCENT (WITH HER VOLUPTUOUS BUST ON DISPLAY) TO WIN MY FATHER'S HEART.

MY MOTHER WAS THE "TISSUE TEX" MODEL. IT WAS THE NEW FABRIC OUT.

TURNING TO HIS FRIEND, HE SAID, "I'M GOING TO MARRY HER..."

THESE PHOTOS WERE TAKEN WHEN MY PARENTS WERE FIRST MARRIED.

LOOK HOW YOUNG, CHARMING, BEAUTIFUL AND ELEGANT MY MOM LOOKS!

SHE GIVES 100% AND IS ADORED 110%.

18

...AND HE DID!

ON DECEMBER 5TH, 1947, THE TWO MARRIED, AND THEY ARE STILL MARRIED TO THIS DAY!

MY DAD SAID, "THIS IS THE FACE I'VE BEEN DRAWING MY ENTIRE LIFE!"

MOM SURE KNOWS HOW TO PICK 'EM! DAD
ALWAYS EMULATED ERROL FLYNN AND
CARY GRANT, ADMIRED BECAUSE OF THEIR
ELEGANCE AND TASTE.

HANDSOME AND UNDERSTATED, HE WAS A
REAL CHARMER. HE DROVE WOMEN WILD...
REAL EYE CANDY!

LOOK AT HOW PHOTOGENIC THEY BOTH ARE!
THEY WERE MEANT TO BE OUT IN PUBLIC,
BUT OFTEN PREFERRED TO SPEND TIME AT
HOME (WITH ME). WE HAD A VERY HAPPY
HOME!

MOM WAS ALWAYS A DIVA, LOVING GLAMOUR AND RADIATING FASHION. SHE WAS AN AVANT-GARDE TREND-SETTER BACK WHEN IT WAS TABOO.

DAD LOVED TO SPOIL HER WITH WHATEVER HER HEART WANTED - AND THAT HASN'T CHANGED. DAD REALLY KNOWS HOW TO TAKE CARE OF HIS GIRLS!

DAD ALWAYS LOOKED AT MOM WITH LOVE AND ADORATION. SHE KNOWS JUST WHAT SHE IS DOING!

OKAY, WHICH OF US IS CUTER? REALLY??

GOOD SPORT, DARLING, I KNOW IT'S ME!

I LOVE YOU TOO!

21

AS STAN'S CAREER WAS RAMPING UP, SO WAS MR. AND MRS. LEE'S SOCIAL LIFE.

MOM'S HAIRSTYLE CHANGED MORE OFTEN THAN THE WEATHER. WHATEVER COLOR IT WAS, THAT **WAS** ALWAYS HIS FAVORITE, AND IT BETTER BE MINE!

WHEN WE LIVED IN N.Y., STAN ENJOYED SPENDING TIME WITH HIS BROTHER LARRY, THE ARTIST. NOW THEY LOVE TO TALK ON THE PHONE.

PARENTS WITH SANDRA THE HAT MODEL.

STAN WAS ALWAYS WORKING, BUT HE ALSO KNEW HOW TO HAVE FUN - HE AND MOM ENJOYED ONE HELL OF A GOOD TIME TOGETHER AND STILL DO. MY MOTHER CLOSED DOWN ALL THE BARS, AND MY FATHER, NOT DRINKING, HAD THE BEST TIME OF EVERYONE.

STAN WITH KATE BOLT, SUCCESSFUL ACTRESS WITH ARTIST HUSBAND - STILL DEAR FRIENDS TO THIS DAY AND TWO OF MY FAVORITE FAMILY FRIENDS...

STAN LOVES HIS RIDES...AND HE LOVES THEM SMOOTH. (AND SOMETIMES A LITTLE FLASH DOESN'T HURT!)

GOOD PURCHASE, STAN, BUT YOU BOUGHT IT FOR YOUR WIFE AND SHE ENJOYED DRIVING IT. YOU GO, GAL!

THE LEES HAVE ALWAYS LOVED THEIR CARS. BACK THEN WOMEN DIDN'T USUALLY DRIVE, BUT WHEN SHE'S GOT A *ROLLS*, NO ONE CAN STOP MOM FROM TAKING IT OUT FOR A SPIN!

THE GANG'S ALL HERE!

STORIES FROM STAN AND JOAN'S CREW...

SANDRA POPE, JOAN'S BEST FRIEND AND FELLOW HAT MODEL. THESE TWO LOVED NOTHING MORE THAN TO SMILE- *AND SHOP!*

WHEN SANDRA MARRIED THE NATIONAL ENQUIRER'S OWNER/PUBLISHER GENE POPE, HE TOLD HER: "YOU WILL NEVER SPEAK TO JOAN AGAIN." SHE DIDN'T...UNTIL THE DIVORCE.

SANDRA WAS A GENEROUS AND BEAUTIFUL GOD-MOTHER TO ME. GRACEFUL AND STATUESQUE.

GENE POPE SAW SANDRA WALKING POOL-SIDE AT THE FOUNTAIN BLUE IN MIAMI AND THAT WAS IT!

THEN CAME THE EMERALD ENGAGEMENT RING.

STAN AND JOAN'S DEAREST FRIENDS, MURRAY AND DOROTHY PLATT, ALL AT THE EL MOROCCO.

THE PLATTS LOVE MY PARENTS. THEY HAD A HOUSE ON DUNE ROAD IN WEST HAMPTON BACK WHEN IT WAS ONLY KNOWN TO FISHERMEN. MURRAY PLATT MADE A FORTUNE IN SOFTWARE EVEN BEFORE MOST OF THE WORLD HAD HEARD OF COMPUTERS. EVERY SUMMER THEY WENT TO FRANCE FOR TWO MONTHS - WITH THEIR DOGS, JEWELS AND STAFF!

MOM AND DAD WERE ALWAYS MEMBERS OF THE MOST FASHIONABLE PRIVATE CLUBS. THE NIGHT LIFE HAS LESS APPEAL THESE DAYS, BUT MOM AND DAD ARE STILL MEMBERS OF SOME PRIVATE CLUBS IN LA. MY MOTHER ALWAYS LIT UP THE ROOM - MEN STILL FIGHT TO BE NEAR HER BECAUSE SHE IS HAPPY, LOVED AND WANTS FOR NOTHING. MEN CAN SENSE THAT.... **WHAT A STAR!**

LOOK AT MY FATHER, THE HAPPIEST MAN ALIVE. WHO WOULDN'T BE?

HE'S ALWAYS HAPPY WHEN SHE'S AROUND. (ALSO - CHECK OUT THAT FABRIC!)

26

SANDY AND THE GREATEST MOM, JOAN.

BOY, CAN THEY STRIKE A POSE!

JOAN'S FATHER, NORMAN DUNTON BOOCOCK, CAME FROM A WEALTHY FAMILY, BUT HE GAVE UP EVERYTHING TO MARRY THE LOVE OF HIS LIFE - HANNAH.

HE WAS THE MOST GENTLE OF MEN. HE
SPOILED HANNAH WILDLY AND DID ALL THE
COOKING SO HANNAH COULD GET HER BEAUTY
SLEEP - QUITE A FEAT IN THOSE DAYS!

MY BEAUTIFUL GRANDMA HANNAH. SHE WAS
ALWAYS KNITTING, SMOKING AND SMILING.
SHE HANDMADE MY SWEATERS, DOLLS AND
PURSES. EVERYONE WANTED WHAT MY
GRANDMOTHER MADE. THERE IS NOTHING
LIKE ONE-OF-A-KIND CLOTHES THAT EVERYONE
WISHES THEY COULD WEAR. I LOVED EVERY
STITCH, GRANDMA.

SHE WAS ALSO VERY PSYCHIC. WHENEVER
I WAS IN TROUBLE, SHE WOULD GET A
PREMONITION AND CALL MY MOTHER -
BECAUSE SHE KNEW!

SUCH A WARM AND LOVING GRAND-
MOTHER. I WISH SHE HADN'T LIVED AN
OCEAN AWAY. NO ONE WOULD'VE TAKEN
ADVANTAGE OF ME HAD SHE BEEN HERE.

MY GRANDFATHER, MOTHER'S SISTER, HER HUSBAND, MY GRANDMOTHER AND THEIR SON JOHN. I WISH WE WERE ALL TOGETHER NOW.

MY COUSIN JOHN HAD THE COMIC BOOK COLLECTION. MY GRANDMOTHER IS IN THE DARK SWEATER, AND MY GRANDFATHER IN THE BLACK PANTS. THAT'S HIS MOTHER AND FATHER IN BETWEEN. I LOVE MY FAMILY IN NEWCASTLE.

MY MOTHER WITH HER SISTER NORMA AND HUSBAND HENRY.

NORMA AND HENRY LOVED TO DANCE. WHEN THEY DANCED IT WAS LIKE NO ONE ELSE WAS IN THE ROOM. I ADORED THEM BOTH!

HENRY OWNED A LARGE CAR DEALERSHIP, SO NORMA DROVE A NEW CORVETTE EVERY YEAR.

NORMA LOVED HORSEBACK RIDING AND COULD JUMP WITHOUT HITTING THE BARS. HER FIRST HUSBAND OWNED A HORSE RANCH IN CANADA AND WAS APPROACHED BY WALT DISNEY, WHO WANTED TO SELL HIM MICKEY AND MINNIE MOUSE. HE ASKED WALT, "WHO THE HELL WANTS TO BUY A MOUSE?" SHE PLAYED PIANO AND LOVED TO BE IN PARADES ON HORSEBACK. SHE MADE A HUGE NEEDLEPOINT OF SPIDER-MAN THAT IS IN MY DAD'S OFFICE TODAY. SHE WAS CREATIVE AND BEAUTIFUL.

NEXT UP...

1950. THE YEAR OF PINK AND TOYS.

I WAS NAMED JOAN AFTER MY MOTHER. MY MIDDLE NAME CELIA IS AFTER MY FATHER'S MOTHER. AND MY LAST NAME LEE...WELL THAT'S A STORY IN ITSELF. ALL GOOD, NO PROBLEM. I WAS WELCOMED INTO THIS WORLD WITH A MOTHER SO THRILLED TO HAVE ME. AND ONCE I WAS BORN THERE WAS NO STOPPING ME!

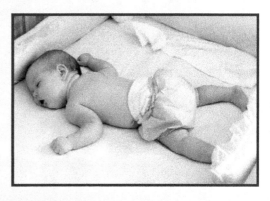

MOM, JOAN LEE, WAS SO EXCITED WHEN SHE FOUND OUT SHE WAS HAVING A LITTLE GIRL THAT SHE PAINTED HER AND DAD'S TWO-STORY LONG ISLAND HOME *BRIGHT PINK*...

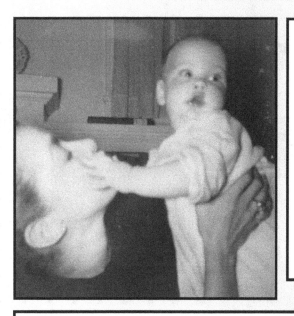

...JUST IN CASE THERE WAS ONE PERSON IN THE STATE OF NEW YORK WHO HADN'T HEARD THE GOOD NEWS, HERE IT IS AGAIN! THIS LOVE AFFAIR DIDN'T NEED ME... BUT I'M SO GLAD THEY INVITED ME IN!

MY GRANDMOTHER ALWAYS SAID I HAD BIG EARS. MY MOTHER IS HIDING THEM WITH THAT CRAZY SCARF!

MOM'S FAVORITE FOUR-LEGGED GUY, HECUBA.

37

AS MUCH AS I WANTED BROTHERS AND SISTERS, I LOVED NOT SHARING MY MOMMY! AND YOU THINK I WANTED TO SHARE MY DAD?

I STILL LOVE MY MOTHER DEARLY. I'M ALWAYS CALLING HER. I LOVE OUR TIME TOGETHER AND WISH SHE AND DAD WEREN'T SO BUSY. HOW GENEROUS OF ME TO SHARE THEM WITH THE WHOLE WORLD.

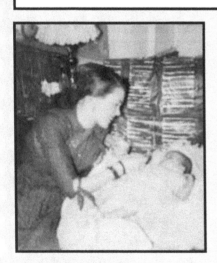

IT'S NOT EASY! THE WORLD IS A DEMANDING, HUNGRY BEAST!

DAD HAD ALWAYS SPOILED MOM WITH LOVE AND GIFTS. MAGNIFY THAT BY TEN AND THAT'S HOW SPOILED I WAS.

THANKS TO ALL THE DOLLS, COSTUMES AND LATEST AND CRAZIEST TOYS THAT I GOT, FAO SCHWARTZ KNEW ME **BY NAME.**

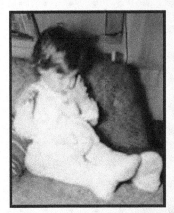

IT DIDN'T HELP THAT THEIR STORE WAS RIGHT ACROSS FROM DAD'S OFFICE. SOMETIMES I THINK THEY MOVED THERE **BECAUSE THEY KNEW STAN LEE JUST HAD A KID.**

MY FIRST
TIME WITH A
PROFESSIONAL
PHOTOGRAPHER.

GOSH, I
DID GOOD!

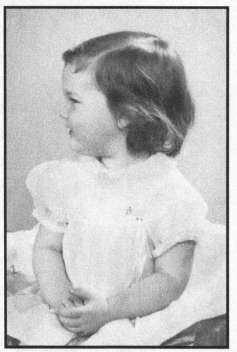

WE LEES DON'T LOVE THE CAMERA AT ALL, DO WE?

1953: TRAGEDY.

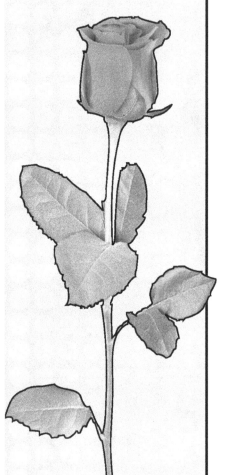

MY MOTHER WAS HOPING TO HAVE MORE CHILDREN, BUT MY YOUNGER SISTER JAN DIED SHORTLY AFTER SHE WAS BORN. POOR LITTLE INFANT WAS SO TINY.

MOTHER WAS UNABLE TO GIVE BIRTH AFTERWARDS. STILL WANTING TO HAVE SIBLINGS FOR THEIR ONLY DAUGHTER, MY PARENTS TRIED THE ADOPTION ROUTE, BUT BACK THEN IT WAS VERY DIFFICULT FOR A JEWISH-AMERICAN MARRIED TO A BRITISH WOMAN RAISED IN THE CHURCH OF ENGLAND TO ADOPT.

SO LUCKY WE ALL LOVED DOGS! AND LUCKY I LOVED CRAYONS AND ALL THE GOOD STUFF.

42

THE WHEEL KEEPS ON TURNING.

WE WISHED THERE WERE MORE LEES SO WE COULD SHARE OUR LOVE, BUT WE WERE STILL A HAPPY FAMILY. SINCE I WAS AN ONLY CHILD, MOM WAS MY CONSTANT COMPANION AND CLOSEST FRIEND AS WELL AS PERSONAL SHOPPER.

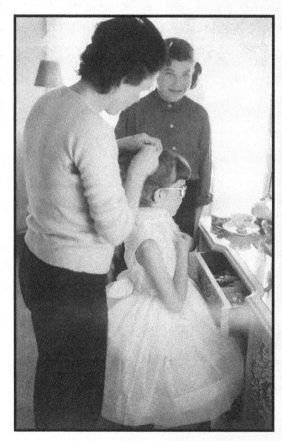

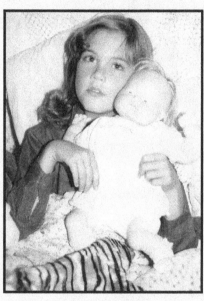

I WAS SPOILED WITH DOLLS, AND WHILE MOST YOUNG GIRLS DURING THAT TIME GREW OUT OF THEIR DOLLS, MINE JUST GOT BIGGER AS I GREW.

STORY-TIME CORNER #1

WHEN I WAS YOUNG, MY PARENTS SAW A
MONKEY PERFORM ON THE ED SULLIVAN
SHOW AND DECIDED THEY WANTED IT AS A
PET. WHAT COULD GO WRONG?

WHEN THEY ARRIVED TO TAKE A LOOK AT
THE MONKEY, HE SKATED INTO THE ROOM
IN A PAIR OF OVERALLS, LOOKING CUTE
AS COULD BE. BUT THEN HE CAUGHT
SIGHT OF MY MOTHER - OR MORE
SPECIFICALLY, HER WELL-ENDOWED CHEST.
HE IMMEDIATELY WENT FOR HER, GRABBING
WITH HIS HANDS.

WE GOT A PARROT INSTEAD.

I WISH I STILL
HAD THESE
COLLECTIBLE
STUFFED
ANIMALS THAT
MY FATHER
DESIGNED.
THEY'RE GREAT!

THERE WAS NO SHORTAGE OF TOYS FOR THIS BABY.

I ALWAYS HAD THE NEWEST AND THE BEST.
THAT IS THE FIRST ELECTRIC CAR IN THE
NEIGHBORHOOD. THAT'S AMY GOODMAN, THE
BOSS'S DAUGHTER, DRIVING ME. MY MOM SAID,
"LOOK AT YOU, YOU WERE ALWAYS MEANT TO
SIT IN THE BACK."

I ALWAYS LOVED PLAYING WITH DOLLS.
I WANTED CHILDREN, BUT THAT HASN'T
HAPPENED. EVEN NOW I WOULD LOVE
SOME LITTLE "DOLLS" TO RAISE.

MIRROR, MIRROR ON THE WALL...I HOPE MY DAUGHTER'S TALL!

STAN LEE AS UNCLE "STAN".

OUR FAMILY HAS A BIG HALLOWEEN PARTY EVERY YEAR.

OH CHRISTMAS. MOM WOULD SPEND HOURS AND HOURS DECORATING THE HOUSE AND BEING THE HOSTESS AT PARTIES.

BIRTHDAYS, HALLOWEEN, CHRISTMAS, EASTER AND EVERY OTHER HOLIDAY, YOU NAME IT, SHE DID IT WITHOUT SPARING ANY EXPENSE...

MOM'S RING IS AS BIG AS THE ORNAMENTS.

TALK ABOUT A GREAT CHRISTMAS! LOVING DANCE, I WAS ALWAYS GIVEN BALLET COSTUMES. I LOVED TO WEAR THEM IN THE HOUSE. SHE LOOKS SO PLEASED AND PROUD. SHE'S ALWAYS DONE THE GREATEST JOB.

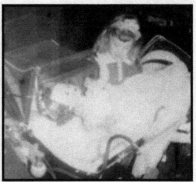

THAT DOLL IS AS BIG AS ME!

I'M STUNNED AT HOW GORGEOUS THIS CARRIAGE IS!

ALL THE NEIGHBORHOOD KIDS WANTED TO PLAY
AT OUR HOUSE. IT WAS FILLED WITH CHARM,
ART, BEAUTY AND SERENDIPITY. THERE WAS NO
OTHER HOME LIKE IT.

A LITTLE PARTY FOR THE LITTLE ONES.

LOOK AT ME UP FRONT, DANCING AROUND.

UH OH! CAUGHT RED-HANDED WITH MY FINGERS IN THE CAKE!

EASTER EGG PARTY!

SAND, SURF, AND LEES

SOME OF MY FONDEST MEMORIES ARE OF THE BEACH. MY PARENTS LOVED THE BEACH. EVERY YEAR WE WOULD VACATION IN FLORIDA.

EVEN THOUGH DAD LOVED THE BEACH, HE STILL WASN'T BIG ON LEAVING HIS BACKYARD.

HE WAS JUST SUCH A WORKAHOLIC, AND WHEN HE HAD TIME OFF, HE'D MUCH RATHER SPEND IT AT HOME THAN ANYWHERE ELSE.

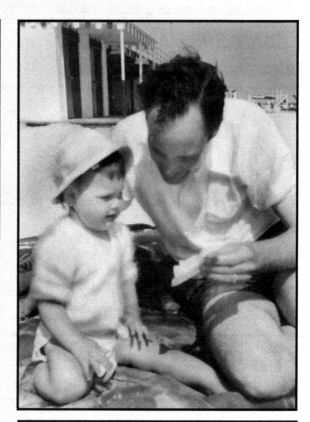

LOOK HOW YOUNG DAD IS!

HERE WE ARE IN MATCHING BATHING SUITS - I LOVED IT WHEN WE DRESSED ALIKE.

MOM, YOU ARE SO DIVINE! WE LEES ARE ALWAYS SO PROUD OF YOU.

BEST THINGS ABOUT THIS BEACH CLUB WERE ITS COCONUT CAKE, ITS MILKSHAKES AND THE FACT THAT MOM USUALLY STOPPED TO BUY ME A NEW DOLL ALONG THE WAY.

WHENEVER WE WERE IN FLORIDA, I WOULD DRAG DAD TO THE MONKEY ZOO OR TO WATCH CROCODILE WRESTLING...I LOVED IT!

SUPERHEROES AND VILLAINS, EAT YOUR HEART OUT - THIS IS QUALITY TIME!

MY PARENTS AND THEIR LITTLE BLUBBER BALL.

I LOVE THIS PHOTO. I LOVE MY DADDY!

TALK ABOUT GORGEOUS! HE NAILS IT!

STORY-TIME CORNER #2

WHEN I WAS A KID,
I HAD TO WEAR AN
EYEPATCH FOR A WHILE,
AND I ABSOLUTELY
HATED IT. MOM HAD
THE BRILLIANT IDEA
OF DECORATING THE
PATCH TO MAKE ME
FEEL BETTER, AND IT
WORKED SO WELL THAT
ALL THE KIDS IN THE
NEIGHBORHOOD WANTED
THEIR OWN EYEPATCHES.
THEIR PARENTS GOT SO
FED UP THEY TOLD MOM
TO CUT IT OUT. NO ONE
CAN TELL HER WHAT TO
DO!

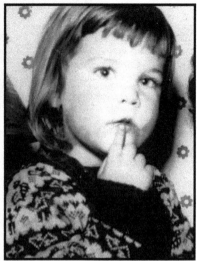

THE LEE DOGS.

MY MOTHER WAS RAISED WITH DOGS AND BELIEVED THAT A CHILD BROUGHT UP WITHOUT DOGS WAS THE SADDEST CHILD IN THE WORLD.

SO NATURALLY WE HAD A LOT OF DOGS OVER THE YEARS. HERE'S JUST SOME OF THEM.

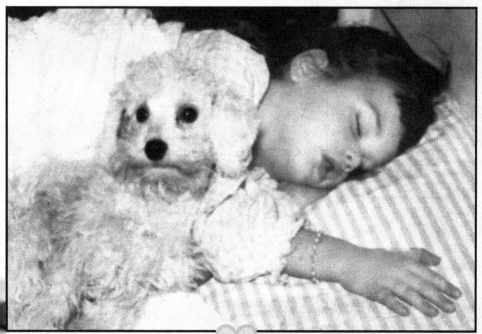

EXCUSE THE FINGERPRINTS, BUT I LOVE THIS PHOTO. THREE DOGS AND A SIDEWAYS CAT IN OUR FAMILY KITCHEN IN HEWLETT HARBOR.

PURE MAGIC, COMING HOME FROM SCHOOL TO MY BABIES!

JENNIE, MY FIRST DOG EVER.

AH, JENNIE. MY PARENTS KEPT HER QUIET IN THE BASEMENT UNTIL I FOUND HER THAT MORNING UNDER THE CHRISTMAS TREE. I NAMED HER JENNIE AFTER THE MOVIE "A PORTRAIT OF JENNIE." WOW, WAS I AHEAD OF MY TIME!

I ALWAYS DRESSED MY BARBIES!

I ALWAYS DRESSED MY DOGS!

JENNIE WAS A TREND-SETTER!

I HAVE A TON OF DOLLS, BUT NOTHING'S MORE FUN TO DRESS THAN DOGS!

63

THIS IS BLACKBERRY, OUR FAMILY PROTECTOR WHEN I WAS LITTLE.

BLACKBERRY AS A PUPPY. HOW WE LOVED THIS DOG!

I COULDN'T MAKE A MOVE WITHOUT HER. SHE'D WALK ME TO THE BUS EVERY MORNING. GOD FORBID ANYONE LOOKED AT ME CROSS-EYED.

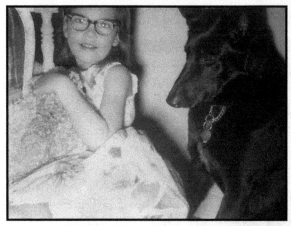

BACK THEN
BLACKBERRY
COULD BE
AGGRESSIVE.
SHE WAS MY
PROTECTOR –
STAN MADE
SURE OF IT.

BLACKBERRY
WAS MY BEST
FRIEND.

DAD WAS MY HANDSOME HERO. SURROUNDED BY DOGS AND ART SUPPLIES, I'D EAGERLY WAIT FOR HIM TO COME HOME. THAT WAS THE BEST MOMENT OF THE DAY, BESIDES WAKING UP TO MOM.

I LOVE THIS PHOTO. WHAT COULD BE BETTER THAN BEING HELD IN MY DADDY'S ARMS AND HAVING MY GRANDMOTHER THERE AS WELL? THERE IS NOTHING LIKE A GRANDMOTHER. I WISH SHE WAS HERE NOW.

THE LEES LOVE THEIR DOGS. I DIDN'T GET
BROTHERS OR SISTERS, JUST DOGS. AS LONG
AS I HAD DOGS AROUND MY PARENTS FELT I
WAS HAPPY AND OKAY. THEY WERE RIGHT!

HE WAS A CREATIVE GENIUS WHO NEVER STOPPED WORKING, BUT HE ALWAYS FOUND TIME FOR ME. WHAT A PRIVILEGE TO HAVE THE DEVOTION, ATTENTION AND LOYALTY OF THE GREATEST AMERICAN ARTIST ALIVE. THANK YOU, DAD - YOU RULE!

IT WAS EASY TO SING WITH MY DAD NEXT TO ME.

COME CLOSER, I DON'T WANT TO YELL.

PAY ATTENTION!

I LOVE GIVING MOMMY AND DADDY GOOD ADVICE. IF ONLY THEY LISTENED!

ALWAYS LOVING MOMMY!

I MIGHT NOT HAVE HAD SISTERS, BUT I HAD GOOD PROPS.

DADDY, ONE DAY YOU'RE GOING TO BE THE MOST FAVORITE COMIC BOOK WRITER IN THE WORLD, AND EVERYONE WILL LOVE YOU AS I DO NOW.

LOOK HOW GORGEOUS SHE IS! I MUST SAY
MOTHER WAS NOT IN THE KITCHEN MUCH.
SHE LOVED TO DECORATE, SOCIALIZE AND
ENJOY HER HOUSE. WE HAD HELP WHO
ACTUALLY RAN THE KITCHEN, BUT MOM DID
COOK A MEAN STEAK! IN HER SIXTIES OR SO,
SHE REDID HER KITCHEN. AND CAN SHE COOK?
WHAT? YOU DOUBT HER? NEVER. LOOK AT
THAT FACE. P.S. SHE'S NOT A BAKER.

DADDY ALWAYS ENJOYED HIS PERSONALIZED LICENSE PLATES, HIS CARS, HIS PARKING SPOTS AND HIS SUPER-HEROES. HE ALWAYS LOOKS GREAT FOR THE CAMERA.

NOTHING COULD STOP THESE TWO!

ISN'T THIS MAGICAL?

LOOKING FOR A FOUR-LEAF CLOVER.

THE DUCK POND IN HEWLETT HARBOR IS MY FAVORITE PLACE. IF I DIDN'T GO THERE EVERY DAY, I CERTAINLY WANTED TO. ALL LEFTOVER BREAD WENT TO THE DUCKS. TO THIS DAY, I HAVE NEVER EATEN A DUCK!

HAPPY WITH MY WEB-FOOTED FRIENDS!

73

I WISH WE STILL HAD THIS VANITY - A PETER HUNT. IT WOULD BE WORTH A FORTUNE NOW.

MOTHER WAS ALWAYS AHEAD OF HER TIME AND KNEW HER ART.

MOMMY AND I WERE ALWAYS SO GIRLY. WE COULDN'T HAVE ENOUGH MAKE-UP, PERFUME AND ACCESSORIES. STILL CAN'T.

THE LEE LADIES HIGH-FIVE TO HANDBAGS. YOU SHOULD SEE OUR COLLECTION.

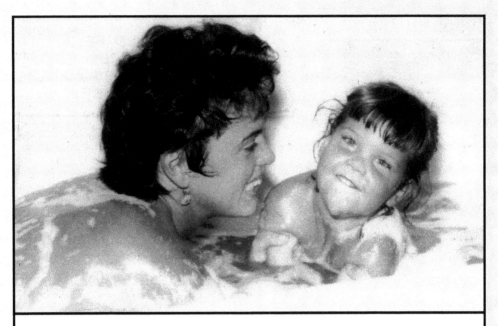

BECAUSE I WAS AN ONLY CHILD, MY MOTHER
WAS MY CONSTANT COMPANION AND
CLOSEST FRIEND. MY MOM ALMOST DIDN'T
SURVIVE MY BIRTH. THE DOCTORS TOLD
HER NOT TO HAVE ME, BUT MOM SAID NO
WAY. SHE WAS BEDRIDDEN FOR MOST OF HER
PREGNANCY, IN PAIN, BUT SHE WANTED ME
THAT BADLY. THANK YOU, MOM.

DADDY WOULD BE IN THESE PICTURES TOO, BUT SOMEONE HAD TO HOLD THE CAMERA!

BETWEEN THAT FACE AND THOSE BANGS, ONLY A MOTHER COULD LOVE ME.

THANK YOU, MOM!

LOOK AT ME, NAKED AS A JAYBIRD!

KISS KISS, MOMMY!

MORE THAN ANYTHING, MY MOTHER WANTED A DAUGHTER, AND WHEN SHE WAS EXPECTING, SHE WAS THE HAPPIEST LADY IN TOWN.

MY MOTHER'S TEENY, AND I CAME OUT AN ELEPHANT. THE DOCTORS UNWOUND ME WHEN I WAS BORN - THEY THOUGHT I WAS TWINS.

AND I'M STILL YOUR BABY!

UNFORTUNATELY, I HURT MY MOTHER ON THE RIDE. SORRY, MOM!

WE LIVED IN AN AFFLUENT NEIGHBORHOOD. ACROSS THE STREET WAS THE SEAWANE GOLF CLUB, TO WHICH MOST OF OUR NEIGHBORS AND FRIENDS BELONGED.

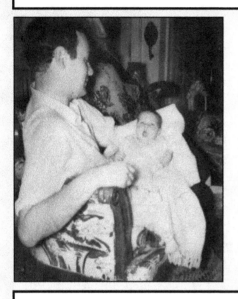 

I TOOK TENNIS LESSONS WHILE DAD PLAYED GOLF. MY FATHER, BEING THE GENIUS WORKAHOLIC THAT HE IS, DIDN'T QUITE HAVE TIME FOR THE SPORT.

MOST OF OUR NEIGHBORS AND FRIENDS WORKED IN THE STOCK MARKET OR THE GARMENT CENTER. OTHERS OWNED HUGE TOY OR CANDY COMPANIES. MY PARENTS WERE THE GLAMOUR COUPLE; THEY WERE THE HOLLYWOOD COUPLE IN A LITTLE TOWN. ALL THE KIDS WANTED THEM TO BE THEIR PARENTS. MY PARENTS WERE THE ONLY ONES IN THE NEIGHBORHOOD WHO DIDN'T DIVORCE. THEY WERE IN LOVE, AND THEY WERE HAPPY. EVERYONE STARES AT THEM, BUT NO ONE UNDERSTANDS. I DO. AND NO ONE ELSE IS SUPPOSED TO. THAT'S WHAT WE CALL FAMILY. BOTH STILL HAVE THE CHARM, THE CHARISMA, THE SUCCESS AND THE BRILLIANCE.

MOMMY WAS MY HAIRDRESSER. UNFORTUNATELY, MY BANGS SUFFERED AT TIMES!

MY DOG BLACKIE WANTS A BATH, TOO! WHEREVER I WAS, HE WANTED TO BE. MY DOGS ARE THE SAME TODAY.

I LOVE THE BATH NOW AS MUCH AS I LOVED THE SINK THEN!

79

THE FAMILY THAT DREAMS TOGETHER...

A LOT OF PEOPLE DON'T KNOW THIS, BUT THE LEES HAVE ALWAYS BEEN A FAMILY OF FAITH. I'M NOT TALKING ABOUT RELIGION, REALLY. I'M JUST TALKING ABOUT LOOKING FOR SOMETHING YOU CAN BELIEVE IN – FAMILY, FRIENDS, DREAM CATCHERS, ANYTHING. I WALK BY FAITH, NOT BY SIGHT.

GRANDMA HANNAH HAD A FINELY TUNED ANTENNA: *THE MOMENT I WAS IN TROUBLE, THE PHONE RANG. SHE KNEW!* SHE'D CALL AND ASK IF I WAS ALRIGHT.

AT 92, MY GRANDMA WAS TOLD SHE WAS GOING TO DIE WITHIN A WEEK. WE WERE SO FRIGHTENED. MY MOTHER GRABBED ME, AND WE RUSHED TO ENGLAND TO SEE HER. THEN GRANDMA DECIDED NOT TO LEAVE SO SOON; *SHE SURVIVED ANOTHER FIVE YEARS.*

HANNAH LIVED FOR MY LETTERS EVERY WEEK. GOD FORBID SHE DIDN'T GET ANY MAIL FROM ME, ALL HELL WOULD BREAK LOOSE. SHE HAS A GREAT MARRIAGE AND A HUSBAND WHO WORSHIPED THE GROUND SHE WALKED ON. MY GRANDFATHER COOKED HIS DAUGHTERS' BREAKFAST AND TOOK THEM TO SCHOOL WHILE GRANDMA HANNAH SLEPT IN. MY MOTHER LEARNED FROM HER – SHE MARRIED A MAN LIKE HER FATHER, A MAN WHO SPOILED HER ROTTEN, TOO! LOOK AT ME, AN OLD MAID WITHOUT A DATE. WHILE THERE'S STILL TIME, I BETTER FIND A MAN TO COOK ME BREAKFAST. THOSE BOOCOCK WOMEN WERE ONTO SOMETHING.

THERE'S NOTHING LIKE THE LOVE AND ACCEPTANCE OF A GRANDMOTHER. GOD BLESS YOU, GRANDMA HANNAH.
MWAH!

I WAS TRAINED TO BE A DANCER. I'VE ALWAYS BEEN GOOD.

MOM STARTED ME IN DANCE WHEN I WAS YOUNG. WE WOULD GO TO BALLET CLASSES TOGETHER. I ALWAYS THOUGHT I WOULD PERFORM WHEN I GREW UP. I WANTED TO ENTERTAIN.

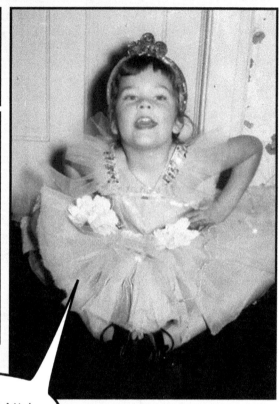

HERE I GO AGAIN WITH MY TUTU!

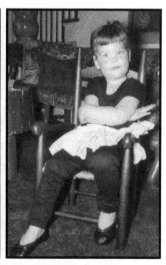

THAT IS MY LITTLE HOUSE IN THE BACKGROUND. ALL THE NEIGHBORHOOD KIDS WOULD COME OVER AND PLAY IN IT. THE LITTLE HOUSE HAD A FIREPLACE, BUNK BEDS AND TOYS.

YES, STAN BOUGHT HER A HOUSE! GOSH HE SPOILS US.

ONE DAY, THE NEIGHBORS' CHILDREN AND THEIR FRIENDS CAME OVER AND DESTROYED MY LITTLE PLAYHOUSE.

IT WAS HURTFUL. I REMEMBER CRYING, BUT IT WAS A GOOD LESSON. PEOPLE ARE JEALOUS. THEY'RE GREEDY. THEY WANT WHAT ISN'T THEIRS, AND THEY'LL DESTROY WHAT THEY CAN'T HAVE. THEY DIDN'T WANT ME TO HAVE SOMETHING THEY DIDN'T HAVE, AND THEY STILL DON'T.

I'VE ALWAYS BEEN INVOLVED IN ART. I ALWAYS HAD A CRAYON, PENCIL, PEN OR BRUSH IN MY HAND. MOM USED TO SAY, "IF YOU TOOK AWAY HER PENCIL, YOU TOOK AWAY HER BREATH." I WENT FROM MAKING WEIRD AND WILD SKETCHES AS A CHILD TO WEIRDER AND WILDER ART AS A TEEN.

MY FAVORITE SPOT WAS IN FRONT OF THE TV WITH PAPER AND ANYTHING THAT I COULD USE TO DRAW - CRAYON, PEN, PENCIL, IT DIDN'T MATTER. I'VE BEEN DRAWING MY WHOLE LIFE.

I DON'T THINK ANYONE SHOULD FEEL THREATENED BY MY ARTISTIC ABILITIES AFTER LOOKING AT THIS PAGE!

WHO'S THE STUDENT HERE? FEELS LIKE I'M CORRECTING HER.

OURS IS A HAPPY PLACE.

PUTTING MY PIECE UP HIGH.

MY BACK STILL HURTS FROM ALL THE PAINTING I DID ON THE FLOOR!

AT SUMMER CAMP, I WOULD MISS MY PARENTS DEARLY, BUT I ALWAYS LOVED MOM'S CARE PACKAGES, ESPECIALLY THE BIG, EXPENSIVE BAGS OF PISTACHIOS.

I HATED BEING APART FROM MY MOM AND MY GORGEOUS DAD WHO CAME HOME EVERY DAY WITH A TOY OR A MALT OR BOTH.

LOVE YOU GUYS!

I WAS ENCOURAGED TO EMULATE MY MOTHER. JOANS WILL BE JOANS. LUCKILY I LOVED IT. WE'RE BOTH A COUPLE OF HAMS AND LOVE THE CAMERA. BUT I APPRECIATE TALENT, AND THAT WOMAN HAS IT. DAD, YOU SHOULD BE FOREVER THANKFUL SHE CHOSE YOU.

87

LIKE ALWAYS, I'M LOOKING UP AT MOM,
AND SHE'S HOLDING ME UP.

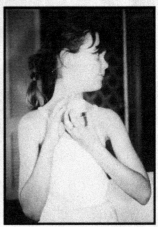

DAD'S TEACHING AND DIRECTING ME AS HE DOES SO WELL. IF ONLY THERE WAS TIME, HE WOULD HAVE BEEN A MASTER FILM DIRECTOR.

I WAS SURROUNDED BY ART AS A CHILD. HOW COULD I NOT BE? MY MOTHER WAS A RARE TALENT AND MY PROLIFIC FATHER STILL TURNS OUT HIS SUPERHEROES. BEHIND EVERY GREAT MAN IS AN EVEN GREATER WOMAN.

YAY, MORE DOGS! ANOTHER BREED - YORKIES. WE LEES LOVE THEM ALL.

LIKE MOMMY AND DADDY - I LOVE YOU TOO, CAMERA!

JOSEPHINE AND HER BABIES!

BETWEEN MOM AND ME, WE HAVE NINE DOGS.

THIS PHOTO WAS TAKEN IN A GAZEBO BESIDE STAN'S OLYMPIC-SIZED SWIMMING POOL.

WHEN SUPERHEROES AREN'T FIGHTING CRIME, THEY'RE HANGING OUT WITH DADDY STAN.

LOOK AT SPIDER-MAN! JEALOUS OF MY
FATHER'S PARKING SPOT.

WHEN MARTIN GAVE DAD THE TASK OF CREATING NEW HEROES, MOM TOLD STAN TO TRY SOMETHING THAT HAS NEVER BEEN DONE BEFORE.

SO DAD DID SOMETHING REALLY RADICAL - HE GAVE HIS SUPERHEROES FLAWS. THAT MADE THEM MORE HUMAN.

ON THE WEEKENDS, DAD LOVED
WORKING OUTDOORS. EVERYONE IN THE
NEIGHBORHOOD WONDERED WHAT AMAZING
STORIES WERE POURING FROM MY FATHER'S
FINGERTIPS AS HE POUNDED AWAY AT THE
KEYBOARD.

LOOK HOW GREAT HE LOOKED WORKING IN
THE SUN. GO DAD!

SEE HOW FATHER IS ALWAYS CONDUCTING WITH
HIS PENCIL. MY FATHER IS A SERIOUS MAN WITH
A FOCUSED VISION. HE WOULD TELL OTHERS
EXACTLY HOW HE WANTED THE COMIC TO LOOK.
HE IS THE GREATEST ART DIRECTOR AND EDITOR.
HE IS ALWAYS THE BOSS. IT IS ALWAYS HIS
VISION.

I LOVE THE ROMITA FAMILY.

STAN WORKING WITH JOHN ROMITA, SR., A GREAT ARTIST AND A GREAT GUY WITH AN EQUALLY GREAT WIFE, VIRGINIA.

99

...AND DAD CREATES A COMMUNITY AROUND COMIC BOOKS.

DAD WASN'T THE ONLY TALENTED ONE IN THE FAMILY. PARAMOUNT WANTED MOM UNDER CONTRACT, BUT THERE WASN'T ENOUGH TIME IN THE DAY AND DAD DIDN'T WANT TO SHARE. SHE GAVE UP CAREER FOR FAMILY.

DAD TELLS EVERYONE, "I MADE A MISTAKE. SHE
SHOULD HAVE BEEN THE ONE WORKING. SHE'S
A CASH COW." BUT SHE GAVE IT UP FOR LOVE.
SHE WANTED TO MAKE SURE WE WERE FED AND
HAPPY, AND THEN SHE BECAME THE WOMAN
BEHIND STAN LEE AND BROUGHT HIM TO THE
TOP WHERE HE BELONGED.

DAD DID A BOOK CALLED "BLUSHING BLURBS."
WHO BETTER TO BE THE STAR OF IT THAN
THE STAR OF HIS LIFE?

NO WONDER HE WAS A GONER!
LOVE AT FIRST SIGHT.

104

MOM HAS ALWAYS LOVED JEWELRY,...

IT HAS BEEN SUCH A PRIVILEGE AND HONOR TO
BE PART OF THE LEE FAMILY, I TREASURE EVERY
MOMENT'S MEMORY. I AM PROUD THAT STAN
AND JOAN B. LEE ARE MY PARENTS. WHAT A
BLESSING. I DON'T BELIEVE THERE IS A MORE
CREATIVE FAMILY ALIVE TODAY. THANK YOU, DEAR
LORD, FOR ALLOWING US TO BE TOGETHER STILL.
BLESSINGS AND GOD BLESS YOU ALL.

ALWAYS,

JC LEE

Excerpt from the Daily Mail Newspaper

The girl who grew up with Spider-Man

JOAN LEE, 20, was brought up in a world inhabited by the super-heroes and villains of American comic strips. Her father edits the exploits of such fantasy creatures as Captain America, Spider-Man, Hulk, Thor and The Fantastic Four.

But despite such alarming early reading, Joan has survived as an attractive and down-to-earth girl. She graduated from the American Academy of Drama last year and has just arrived in London to help her fiancé Isaac Burton-Tigrett, 22, open a <u>new restaurant</u> in Piccadilly.

She also hopes to meet a friend of her father's, Italian film director Federico Fellini.

FIRST
Hard Rock Cafe
Restaurant!

UP NEXT... JC GOES TO ART SCHOOL.

From JC Lee to you...

Thank you. I hope you enjoyed my book.

You've come this far. Please take a look at my paintings and one-of-a-kind jewelry, including the special couture line I created with my mother. We Lee ladies are famous for the jewelry that we wear, design and collect.

I've always loved and wanted a restaurant of my own. Right now I'm working feverishly on "Stan's Super Subs." Look forward to openings in Beverly Hills, Las Vegas and San Diego, so that when my father visits Comic-Con, he'll be able to order his favorite egg salad sandwich whenever he wants.

My new single "Little Baby Jesus" is soon to be released. There is a rock opera in the works – don't hold your breath, I've been working on it since my twenties, but the Gibson is out and Dad is singing along with me. Oh and I almost forgot! I'm working on a new Christian comic that'll be the first in a series about major religions of the world.

I want to make a video of "Little Baby Jesus" with mom and dad performing a duet. They already know the lyrics!

Thanks again. Blessings in all areas.

-JC

FROM *JC LEE'S FATSALAGATA!*

The Lee family tradition continues with JC Lee's new line of products including limited edition hats, prints, clothing, jewelry, music and more!

*See JC's work on the **Fatsalagata.com** website.*

IT'S ALL ABOUT LOVE!

I WAS PLEASED TO SHARE OUR LOVE STORY WITH YOU AND HOPE I GET TO HEAR YOURS. CHECK BACK ON MY WEBSITE *FATSALAGATA.COM* FOR A NEW COMMUNITY FORUM THAT'S ALL ABOUT SHARING LOVE STORIES - *COMING SOON!*